AF599076

The Artist
and
The Storyteller

Goingback and Mary Chiltoskey: A Cherokee Legend

Mary Regina Ulmer Galloway

Mary Regina Ulmer Galloway is the niece of Goingback and Mary Ulmer Chiltoskey. Mrs. Galloway is compiler and editor of **Aunt Mary, Tell Me A Story** (1990), a collection of Cherokee Legends. She lives in Montgomery, Alabama.

Mary Ulmer Chiltoskey is the author of **Cherokee Cooklore: To Make My Bread** (1951), **Cherokee Words with Pictures** (1972), **Cherokee Plants: Their Uses, A 400 Year History**, written with Paul B. Hamel (1975), and **Cherokee Fair & Festival: A History thru 1978** (1979).

Printed by
Cherokee Communications
Cherokee, North Carolina

2618 Aimee Drive
Montgomery, Alabama 36106
334-279-8589

Goingback and Mary demonstrate woodcarving at the 1987 Craftsman's Fair in Asheville. This was the year before G.B.'s heart attack.

The Artist and the Storyteller
Goingback and Mary Chiltoskey: A Cherokee Legend

To Aunt Mary and Uncle G.B. and the people of Cherokee

Introduction

As long as I can remember, my Aunt Mary and Goingback Chiltoskey (who became my uncle when I was 11) have been coming home to West Alabama at Christmas and during summer vacation bringing Cherokee woodcarvings, legends, and baskets. None of us nine cousins can remember a time when we weren't in love with the Cherokee stories and the Cherokee people.

Aunt Mary and Uncle G.B. were such a part of our growing up that it took me many years to understand what an unusual couple they were, how many lives they had awakened, and how much of the Cherokee story might have been lost if not for their influence and farsighted actions. I have been taken with surprise at times to find that Goingback's carvings represent in places all through the United States and Europe the best of Native American sculpture, and Cherokee legends have lived for many thousands in the words of Mary Ellen Ulmer of West Alabama.

Goingback and Mary, married in 1956 against the laws of his native North Carolina, brought together two stubborn cultures: She was born in a log cabin on the banks of the Tombigbee River in Marengo County, Alabama, before there were enough children to have regular schools in the rural areas. He was the tenth child of a Cherokee family who lived up in the Smoky Mountains much as his people had lived for hundreds of years.

At the age of 10, Goingback came down from the mountains to the boarding school at Cherokee, having spoken only the old language all his life. At Cherokee the children were threatened with punishment if they spoke any language except English. G.B. brought his pocket knife and filled silent hours whittling. At the age of 6, Mary left home to live with her grandparents near Demopolis so she could go to school with three other children.

At every point of this story, there were obstacles, but this is not a story of troubles because G.B. and Mary have never allowed obstacles. The many, many people who have encountered them have seen a story of possibilities and determination. A visit to the Chiltoskey home between the Oconaluftee River and Rattlesnake Mountain in Cherokee is a brush with fascination embodied in the old stories and the warm woodcarvings and the two faces of strong security.

I think of this little biography as one of the legends still being lived on the Qualla Boundary.

Many people helped with this labor of love. I would like to thank Vickie Sequoyah McCoy, Gene Jackson, and Hugh Lambert of Cherokee; and the many artists, photographers and journalists who have documented the unusual Chiltoskey story over the last half century. I appreciate, too, those in my family who have shared memories and much support: Johnny, Cole and Bart Galloway, Nellie Ulmer, M.B. Ulmer, Jr., Susan Ulmer Wallace, and Clara Tucker. G.B.'s colleagues in Washington were quite helpful, especially Bert Swenson.

Will and Charlotte pose with G.B. and his older brother Watty. (Picture taken in 1910)

High in the Smoky Mountains

"I will lift up mine eyes unto the hills"

Psalm 121 1:2

His Cherokee name is Utsvdv Tsiladoosgi (ᎤᏨᏛ ᏥᎳᏙᏍᎩ); the modern Cherokee people speak English and call him Goingback Chiltoskey. His wife Mary calls him G.B. Chiltoskey is said to mean Falling Flower, which may be connected to the idea of the time of fertility.

A family story tells that G.B.'s grandfather was one of the Cherokee people driven to the West during the removal, the infamous Trail of Tears. The older Chiltoskey was so unhappy and homesick that he often talked of plans to go back to the mountains. In time he did return, and according to the legend, Will named his youngest son Goingback in tribute to the stubborn strength of his people.

G.B. says he does not remember anything about his grandfather. He told a reporter for the Charlotte *Observer* (2-8-72) that memory of the Trail of Tears "will never die out. It will always be remembered by the Indians. They will never forget and neither will anyone else who knows anything about it."

Goingback Chiltoskey was born in the Smoky Mountains near Cherokee, North Carolina, on April 20, 1907, the tenth and last child of Charlotte Hornbuckle and Will Chiltoskey. G.B. remembers his brothers Ute and Watty and his sister Nancy, but he only heard stories of the older children who had died before he was born. His parents spoke Cherokee, and he spoke only the old language until he was ten. After the family moved to Big Witch when he was 6, he remembers his father carrying him seven miles across the mountain when there were no roads into the mountains.

One of G.B.'s earliest memories is his older brother Watty carving and letting him learn to whittle with a new pocket knife Watty gave him. Watty and Goingback would remain close and work together at times during a long life until Watty's death in 1973.

Charlotte Chiltoskey spoke only Cherokee all of her life. She was a strong woman who taught her children to obey authority. Charlotte was expert in using the old medicines of the body and the soul. G.B. tells of a time during the national influenza epidemic of 1917-18 when his mother saved their family with one of the traditional remedies learned from her people.

So many people were dying of influenza around the area of the Qualla Boundary, as around the country, that the horror stories still are told today. One mother is said to have been found several days dead still holding a nursing baby in her arms. The Will Chiltoskey family faced almost certain suffering and death. Goingback remembers that his mother called everyone into their house and instructed the boys to bring fresh pine branches for the fire. They closed the house up tight and burned the resin-filled pine. No one of the Chiltoskey family was sick from the rampant disease for more than two days!

The Bicentennial volume *Mothers of Achievement in American Histo.* features Charlotte as one of the outstanding mothers from North Carolina. Th say the Chiltoskey children "owed their existence to their mother's use of plan that grew around their house" (404). They also cite her expertise in food prepar tion. Years after her death, G.B. and Mary worked together to publish books c Cherokee cooking and use of medicinal plants. Charlotte, I think, would hav been amazed to find herself selected an outstanding American mother during tl bicentennial of the United States, and she would have been quite pleased with h son's input into the books that have preserved much of the old culture.

When G.B. was still the Cherokee blowgun champion in his seventies, h was using a blowgun handed down from over 100 years before. He remembe learning to use the blowgun to hunt small animals when he lived high in th mountains.

Cherokee Boarding School

When Goingback was ten, two truant officers Twister Littlejohn and Will Wayahneta were hired to find the children up in the mountains who needed to be in school. These officials, who were hired around the time of the terrible flu epidemic, found G.B. one day near his home at the forks of Wrights Creek and Big Witch and "took him down to the boarding school at Cherokee."

G.B. told Mrs. Thomas Blossom in a 1941 interview that he was not happy at first at the English-speaking school. Mrs Blossom writes, "It wasn't very long before (he) was back home from school. Twister came and got him again, and again (he) ran home." G.B. prefers now to remember the value of his learning at the boarding school, even though some of the treatment may be seen as harsh. He tells of his pride at getting along with people and having them accept him. According to G.B., "They treated me as well as I wanted to be treated, and didn't have any prejudice against me in any way I knew of. But you could get it right away if you wanted it" (*Foxfire*, Fall 1983, 172).

Mary has researched the early mountain schools. She explains that after the Civil War ended, churches around the country grew concerned about the many children from isolated areas who had no formal schooling. It had been all too evident to people who observed the very young boys who were the soldiers in that tortuous four year war that the youngsters needed education. Most of the schools that came from this movement were boarding schools because there were as yet no roads into the mountains and other isolated areas of this country.

In the summer of 1875 Enola Blackfox of Cherokee told visiting journalist Rebecca Harding Davis of *Lippincott Magazine* about the origin of the boarding school. When members of the Friends (Quakers) met for their Western Yearly Meeting in Indiana, one of the isolated areas discussed was the Smoky Mountain area in Tennessee and North Carolina. Two doctors Mr. and Mrs. D. Garner were sent to Maryville, Tennessee, to study the situation. From the family of Aggie Lossiah, great-granddaughter of Chief John Ross, who were living in a cave in the area, the doctors learned of the Cherokee families across the mountains on the Qualla Boundary.

A member of the Friends, Barnabas Hobbs, came to Big Cove near Cherokee and found children in need of schooling. Hobbs also found mica deposits enough to sell to fund the efforts at least for a time.

A Chiltoskey family story tells of Will, G.B.'s father, going to school for one week. Mary says that Will probably really wanted to stay in school. She thinks that Will found a situation which was not unusual. Stories say that for the first terms of the school at Cherokee, young teachers would begin the term, but they would leave for Asheville after the first paycheck, and they would not come back. Possibly Will went to school for a week, and he returned after the weekend with a relative nearer to the village than his home to find the teacher gone - again, no school.

At the Bureau of Indian Affairs boarding school, which by 1917 had been taken over by the Federal Government, Goingback lived in the boys dorm, where the boys were to speak only in English, a language he had hardly even heard before. He tells about having trouble understanding the instructions he was given. Punishments, including washing out the students' mouths with soap and being locked in or sent to their rooms, were used if the students did not speak English. G.B. remembers taking his pocket knife and going out in the woods with some of the other boys so they could whittle and talk in the old language and rest a little from the new demands.

Gene Jackson told *Foxfire* reporters (Fall 1983), "The school was maintained in a military fashion ..... If the young ladies wore long hair when they were admitted, it was automatically cut off - because of lice they assumed we had. We were lined up and bathed like animals, not in private." (171)

Hugh Lambert, who was sent to the boarding school at six years old after his mother's death, also remembers a school run like the military. As a little boy, he saw marshals with guns and on horseback bring back runaway students to face time in "jail," shaved heads, and escorts to class. Walker Calhoun and G.B. may have been some of these runaways. The marshals with the Colt 45's were the truant officers, whom Gene Jackson remembers as "tough men."

The school day was divided into a session of morning classes and afternoon work hours, alternated with a session of morning work and afternoon classes. The students studied half a day; then they applied themselves to practical tasks such as building a stone wall that still stands near the Festival Grounds in Cherokee today.

The boarding school offered classes through the ninth grade. The Chiltoskeys lived off the land, so they had no money to help G.B. He had to find ways to earn what little money he needed. Early on, he learned he could carve things that people valued and which they would buy. G.B. remembers that when some people in the village got new Model T cars, short journeys became possible if you could scrape up the little money it took. After his required work for the school, he made wood carvings to sell. Years later, Hugh Lambert's teacher in Cherokee High School wood carving class was Goingback Chiltoskey.

High School and Snake Handling

After completing the ninth grade in 1927, Goingback went to Parker High School in Greenville, South Carolina, for more high school training. Parker had a reputation for a good program in woodworking. G.B. says he was fortunate to find a family in the Greenville neighborhood with whom he could live.

He found odd jobs in his four years at Parker, and, again, he found that people liked his carvings enough to buy them. He remembers feeling more at ease with the English language during these years, and he says people were nice to him. When he looks back, he sees good work and unusual possibilities; he has enjoyed his accomplishments. Half a century after his Parker High years, he told a *Foxfire* reporter, "A short time ago there was somebody visiting [Cherokee] from Greenville and she said the family that I had boarded with was still showing with pride the cedar chest I made for the mother" (Fall 1983, 172).

In 1931, G.B. had to leave his work at Parker and take a job at a cotton mill. The Great Depression was gripping the country, and he had to earn money however he could. He remembers that he was the "only Indian in town," and some of the citizens of Greenville seemed afraid of him, afraid that he would "turn wild." One day after work in Greenville, Goingback ran into a fellow setting up a side show of reptiles. The man asked if he wanted to put a snake around his neck and hawk the show to help sell tickets. So G.B. became a snake handler in a traveling reptile show!

The way G.B. tells it, he was out of high school, looking for a job, and he came across this guy with a reptile show, an old fashioned side show. So he learned to handle snakes. What could be more natural?

The show traveled to Charlotte, North Carolina; Richmond, Virginia; and finally to Washington, D.C. In D.C. a boy came to the show and asked G.B. if he knew anything about American Indian beadwork. G.B. had learned beadwork from Watty and agreed to teach the young man. They became fast friends, and the boy invited G.B. to come to work at his home. About this time, the snake handling job was running into problems. The sideshow man had promised G.B. a little money, a clothes allowance, and food, but the show ran out of money, and the promises were not kept. In the meantime the beadwork boy and G.B. were making beaded items "like crazy" and they were selling. So G.B. turned again to his native crafts to make his way for him.

During this time G.B. went to the office of the Bureau of Indian Affairs in Washington to ask about the possibility of going to school at Haskell Institute in Lawrence, Kansas, a tribal school established in 1884 for American Indian students. He was told that he could get into Haskell, but a deadline had passed which would have provided transportation, so he had to earn his own way out to Kansas.

G.B. left Washington, traveled to Cherokee for a visit, and left again for Lawrence, Kansas. When he arrived at Haskell, he ran into a close boyhood friend from Cherokee named George Washington. G.B. and George had grown up together and had been on the same basketball team. George's brother had married G.B.'s niece. George helped him get settled at Haskell, and G.B. began his studies again.

No one in Washington, D.C., could have guessed that the Indian snake handler would return to be a master carver and model-maker for the United States Corps of Engineers.

Born to Teach

"On the Tombigbee River so bright I was born . . ."

Southern folk song

Mary Ellen Ulmer was born on January 13, 1907, in a log cabin near the Tombigbee River in Marengo County, Alabama. She was the oldest of the five girls and two boys to be born to Mary Nettie Lipscomb and Edward Warham Ulmer. Nettie and Ed farmed a large tract of river land 10 miles form Demopolis on the Moscow Road. Ever the numbers lady, Mary remembers measuring the distance with Ulmer's first automobile, a used Oakland they bought from Mrs. Marshall Shackleford of Demopolis.

Mary says she was born to be a teacher. She interprets as life-long lessons some of her early experiences. One episode she still uses to instruct those around her involves a time a black man slapped her. Of course, in Alabama in the 1920s, this could have been an explosive situation. But, she stresses, you have to know the whole story: Mary and Larry, her oldest brother, were playing too near the river when the man, who was a longtime family friend, had to act fast. He literally slapped her away from the riverbank and probably saved her life. Millard, her baby brother and my father, told us about hearing Mary's lessons long before he ever went to school.

Her earliest memories stay with her as lessons from her parents. She remembers a time before she was three years old. Her mother had made a cake and she wanted a piece. Her mother said she would have to wait. She huffed and puffed and fumed and finally, with her little purse in her hand, she ran away from home. Not far from her porch was a mama hog and her little pigs. Mary was so afraid of the hog that she dropped her little purse and ran home, and learned to wait for the cake.

Another early lesson involved sharing. Mary had some crayons, a rare possession in those days. She did not want the little brothers and sisters to share the crayons because she just knew they would get broken. When she was asked for the crayons, she skirted the issue by repeating a little ditty which was popular with the girls she knew:

"Robert E. Lee had a flea
Jumped in the river and tee hee hee."

This little saying seemed to get the other girls our of situations when they didn't want to answer. For example, if a girl hadn't had much of a weekend, she might coyly use the chant.

Mary's mother passed by just as she was repeating the verse to one of the other children and asked, "What did you say?"

"Nothing."

Her mother went on about her work, and Mary froze in her tracks. "Wha does that mean?" her mother asked after a long pause.

Mary answered, "It doesn't mean anything. We just say it. I don't know what it means."

"**From now on**," said her mother, "**when you make a statement, be sur you at least think you know what it means. If not, have the good sense to ask question and get some help.**"

Those of us who were raised around Mary and her mother (our D.D. Mama know well that certain way of saying something that you are not likely to forget They do not raise their voices, but you never forget what they said.

Nettie and Ed pose with (l-r) Mary, 5 years old, Larry, and Kitty. (Picture taken February 28, 1912)

Lessons and Stories

Not long before Goingback was coming down from the Smokies to learn nglish and begin school, Mary left the farm on the Moscow Road to go closer to own to school. She moved in with her Lipscomb grandparents, her great-randmother, and her Aunt Clara (who was only 14 months older) to be one of the our children to attend the Patterson School at the Lipscomb home near emopolis. In another bit of foreshadowing, she now thinks this was the first chool in Marengo County to have a library.

Mary's first teacher at the country school was Mr. Larkin Eddins, also the irst wonderful storyteller she remembers. Ironically, among the Greek and oman stories, Mr. Larkin told her a Cherokee legend. It was the legend of the herokee rose sent by the the Great Spirit to mark the Trail of Tears during the rutal removal of the Cherokee to the West. In Marengo County, Alabama, the armers knew well the staying power of the Cherokee rose. No one yet guessed a arengo County girl would help save the culuture of the Cherokee in books, as heir teacher, and as their storyteller.

When it was time for eighth grade, Mary had to move again, this time into emopolis to live with some aunts and attend Demopolis High School. Until ighth grade, Mary's classes had been near her grandparent's home in a school vith only four students. She says this move away to the larger Demopolis school ould have been upsetting except for having relatives all around.

School went fine until she came home with a C- in reading. Report card in and, she approached her father at home that weekend, ready with all the excuses he has since heard many times in more than forty years of teaching. Her father ust looked at the report, which was good except for the reading grade. Then he valked away. Like all students, she figured she had to have his signature before oing back to school, and like all students, she tried to wait until it was time to eave and he was busy. She tiptoed to him, and said, "Poppa, will you sign my eport card. I have to go."

He signed the card, looked down at her and said, "**I expect better of you than hat**." She still hears him say that, over seventy years later.

From the little school in the country, Mary had moved to Demopolis High School. Of the 42 students who started high school with her, 15 graduated on June 1, 1923. In an Asheville *Citizen-Times* interview in 1972, Mary said, "I loved school from the start and never had any doubt as to what I wanted to be -- a school teacher."

The little girl who wanted to be a teacher remembers some shy moments that made her believe she would never be able to speak in front of a group. In the first literary program she participated in at Demopolis, she remembers that her voice broke and everyone giggled. She was so upset that when, on the day of the next program, she broke her nose and had to go home, she was relieved and planned never to be in a program again!

She says it was into the third year of her teaching before she had to stand and present a program again. She was put in charge without warning on a rainy day, and she remembers praying, "Lord, if you let me keep my voice steady this one time, I will always use it to the best advantage." It will be hard for her students and associates who have seen many programs and story-telling sessions to believe that once Mary had a gripping old-fashioned shyness!

Mary says that even after over fifty years of speaking before thousands of groups of people about legends, plants, Cherokee culture, books, quilting, crafts and many other topics, she is still aware at moments of the shy little girl who feels alone and frightened in a crowd. She often thinks of the effect of the little school among relatives and only two or three other students when she hears advocates of home schooling. She would like to question anyone who isolates a child about the realities awaiting them in "a world of strangers."

She remembers that during her senior year her classmate Gussie Mae Charlton and she were discussing their plans after graduation. They knew they didn't have the funds to just go away to college, and they knew there were colleges listed as funded for the rural students of some Alabama counties, but Marengo County was not qualified as the mountain counties were. So they decided to try to go for one summer to Livingston State Teachers College, which was about thirty miles from Demopolis. That way they could get a one-year teaching certificate. They knew that the small Marengo County Schools were slated to be consolidated in the next two or three years. The two aspiring teachers figured they would have a chance at one of the little schools.

Without telling anyone, they sent away the one dollar registration fee and signed up for one summer's work. Mary was hired to teach at the little Moscow School near her home. She was 16 years old and already teaching thirteen students in the little school. Gussie Mae got the school at Dixon's Mill, where she taught her whole career and where she still lives with her husband George Morgan.

The summer Mary got her Normal Diploma (two year degree), some men came through Livingston to recruit teachers to teach in Florida. They made a flowery sales pitch for applicants. All the girls decided to take the opportunity except Mary and one other girl. The two dissenters figured that maybe the costs away from home would offset the gains, and there was no assurance that they would teach in the subject areas they trained in. A dozen girls went to Florida. Ten were home by Christmas, some having gone to communities in which the schools weren't even built! Mary learned to weigh the consequences, but as time would tell, that didn't mean she would stay home in West Alabama.

During the next seventeen years, Mary taught in area schools in Marengo and Sumter Counties while she earned a bachelors degree from Livingston (B.S. 1934) and her masters degree from George Peabody College in Nashville (M.A. 1940).

Cherokee Indian School Class of 1948 with their homeroom teacher Mary Ulmer; back row (l-r) Reginald Thompson, George I. Storm, Mary, William D. Larch, Minnie Queen; middle row - Lavenia Chiltoskie Thompson, Alice Catt Lewis, Charlotte Reed Hornbuckle; front row - Geneva Sneed Jackson, Vivian Bradley McCollough, Mariam Wolfe, Gladys West Parris.

(Picture taken June 2, 1948).

Next Stop, North Carolina

When Mary was a little girl, she remembers insisting to her mother that sh wanted to be an Indian. Her mother at one point told her that she could be a Indian when she got so brave she wouldn't cry when soap got in her eyes. A Peabody in 1940, Mary met Edna Lee Jacobs from Lumberton, North Carolina, th first member of the Lumbee tribe of Indians from Robeson County, North Ca olina, ever to get a college degree. Her interest in Indians grew and grew.

It was still deep Depression years in the the South, and Mary was helping he parents all she could. When she heard from a friend of her roommate at Peabod about a teaching job at the Choctaw reservation in Mississippi, she and her frienc saw an opportunity for teaching positions with the federal government. Thes federal jobs meant year-round employment, and one involved teaching at th Cherokee Indian School in the mountains of North Carolina.

Mary mailed her application for government employment at about the tim the Japanese attacked Pearl Harbor in December, 1941. Weeks went by and, ami the war news and her responsibilities as an elementary principal at the closing c school, she forgot about the application until one day, a letter came which gave he dates to report to North Carolina.

Mary Ellen Ulmer, at the age of 35 and after teaching in rural West Alabam schools for nearly two decades, boarded a train in August, 1942, for the mountair of North Carolina "to give it a try." When I asked Mary's sister Nettie about th family reaction to Mary's taking a train away to an isolated Indian reservatior Nettie said, "I thought she ought to be able to do what she wanted. After all, w were raised to love adventure."

Mary arrived in Cherokee at 1:15 on the afternoon of August 10, 1942. Sh came to the Cherokee Indian Schools to teach math, but very soon she was th history teacher and the librarian. Geneva (Gene) Jackson, a student in Mary's firs homeroom and a longtime friend and companion of the Chiltoskeys, says Mar came to Whittier, North Carolina, that August day. When she looked out the wir dow of the train, the first thing she saw was the state prison grounds. She thougł at that moment that she had until the following Monday to give up her position i West Alabama. If she had to teach at a prison, she might just stay on that train. C course, she was to travel on to Cherokee to teach at the Indian School.

Looking back through the nearly fifty years in Cherokee, Mary remembe that she heard the name Goingback Chiltoskey within twenty hours of arriving i Cherokee. But G.B. had left to take a job with the U.S. Army Corps of Engineers i Washington, D.C., just days before Mary came to the village.

Mary's job was to teach the Indian children, but very soon she knew ther would be more for her to do. She was falling in love with the area, the Cheroke people, and she was noticing one tall woodcarver in particular. She says each tim G.B. came home from Washington, he found some excuse to show her some of hi work and tell her of his life in Washington.

Not long after Mary arrived in Cherokee, Superintendent Joe Jennings asked er to read an Asheville *Citizen* article which Mildred Underwood Blossom had ritten about G.B.'s wood carving and his extraordinary life and education. Mary as to research this Cherokee artist and write an article to be published for his lma mater Haskell Institute in a series called "Indians at Work." She had only et G.B. one time.

Some of her first tasks in Cherokee, however, were far less romantic: She elped can "truck loads of string beans" for winter meals in the boarding school, nd she was assigned to administer the ration coupons for sugar, gasoline, erosene, and flour in the community because this had been one of her respon-ibilities as elementary principal in West Alabama.

Gene remembers that the students in the class of 1948 soon caught on that oingback was a special "friend" of the new teacher from Alabama. They atched the situation develop, and they knew when G.B. made Mary's ebony and lver pin, which she wore as an engagement token. When G.B. left to go back to Vashington, the students understood they were to watch out for Mary. One day ey almost watched too carefully. The class was just about to leave for an ssembly program when a white man they did not know came into the classroom nd grabbed Mary and hugged and kissed her. Gene says the students were just bout to teach this guy who he was dealing with until they noticed through Mary's iggling that she was trying to say, "This is my brother." Mary's sister Alice's usband Charles Woolf had traveled to Cherokee from the military hospital at sheville where he was working during the war.

The Drama Begins

After World War II there began talk of an outdoor drama to be produced t tell the history of the Cherokee. It was hoped that the production would be of th superior quality and success as the Virginia drama *The Lost Colony.* In the wint of 1947, Mary Chiltoskey; Sam Gilliam, principal of the reservation and th Cherokee school; and Irma Mittelberg, music teacher at Cherokee, met to list pos ible episodes from Cherokee history which might be successfully used in an ou door drama. Mary remembers listing several ideas from stories and informatio she had collected since arriving in Cherokee in 1942.

A 1956 Cherokee Historical Association article says that in 1947 a grou organized as the Western North Carolina Associated Communities awaited a vis from Samuel Selden, director of the Carolina Playmakers and one who had bee associated from the beginning with the production of *The Lost Colony.* Durin months of waiting, the writers George Simpson and Harriet Herring speak "perhaps some discouragement" (26). They write, "During this period Miss Mar Ulmer of the Indian School in Cherokee presented a paper on the history of th Cherokee that helped to sustain confidence in the basic story material of th drama" (26).

One of Sam Selden's students was Kermit Hunter. Hunter was given th material that Mary, Mr. Gilliam, and Miss Mittelberg accumulated. The script f *Unto These Hills* was part of his work for his doctorate from the University North Carolina.

Mary remembers the day that she and her longtime friend Molly Arneac Blankenship were the two women who "came over the mountain to pick out th land for the amphitheater." *Unto These Hills* meant jobs, tourist trade, and mo awareness of the Cherokee story for everyone in the region.

The outdoor drama is running still in its forty-second year, drawing crowc from all over the world to learn of the Trail of Tears and the majesty of the Gre Smoky Mountains.

Recently I have read a review that dismissed *Unto These Hills* as one of th old offerings in the Smokies. It seems to me that the story is newer than it has ev been before. We of the fifties generation and later who have been lucky enough experience Cherokee and *Unto These Hills* will need no explanation of mult cultural understanding. We have been there, and we already know how appreciate history - the sad and the joyful - and the differences all the way from th ancestors of the Cherokee. No, the work that began and carries on *Unto Thes Hills* will yield more in the future than was dreamed of in 1947.

Mary had already begun to listen to and collect the legends told her by th older Cherokee people. As a history teacher and librarian, she used stories motivate students (and everyone is Mary's student), and Mary grew up in a famil of storytellers and story-makers. (In fact, she insists that she really is not the pr mier Ulmer storyteller; she says that her sister Alice [our Aunt Duck] knew an told stories from all over the world, a more diverse repetoire than her own.)

Now she was asked by Mr. Gilliam and Joe Jennings to organize a way to ·omote the new drama using the Cherokee legends. She recruited Cherokee udents who formed Legend Clubs to travel to neighboring towns and tell the old ories. Lloyd Arneach, Mollie's son, told me when Mary and I published the 1990 llection of legends that Mary got him started telling the legends of his people just surely as she introduced them to us, her nieces and nephews in West Alabama. oyd was one of those first students to travel with Mary on Saturday mornings to ll the old legends, which many of their listeners had never heard before.

Lloyd, from his home in Atlanta, now does programs about Cherokee history ıd legends all over the state of Georgia, hoping to educate Georgians in the rich- ss and trials of Cherokee culture. Like Mary and G.B., he is modestly and quietly volved in nothing less than saving the knowledge of and respect for Native merican culture.

The drama and the legend group were already history when a sad and sur- ising episode happened one day in the early sixties.

A new principal at the Cherokee school called the teachers together and told em that they were to gather together the Cherokee artifacts, stories, anything ey had amassed of the old ways, and put it outside in a place that had been signated. That afternoon the materials would be burned, and the time used for cluding information and experiences from the old culture would be better used teaching the Cherokee children things they really needed. He based these tions on some Reconstruction Era laws that restricted use of the Native merican languages, rituals, and missionary assignments at the Indian Agency arding schools.

Mary had inherited and accumulated much material about the Cherokee. uth Hollingsworth and Louise Bradford, former teachers at Cherokee, had left aterials for her to use. Several other teachers at the school were using Cherokee aterials to enrich their classes. Mary does not describe the sinking feeling in her art that day, but she does describe the actions she and Opportunities Program acher Nan Tyner took: They found bags and put all their Cherokee treasures refully in the bags. They worked so calmly that no one could have told it was an usual day. She says that since she and Nan usually did stay at school after the quired hours, it was not noticed that they left late and with some packages.

But where could they put the items they were determined to save? They boar- d on the campus, and there was little room for private doings. The decided to de the materials under the boardinghouse beds! It worked. Parts of the Cherokee lture were not burned that day. Mary still considers her actions to be insubor- nate, and she feels very loyal to her employers, but this extraordinary day quired extraordinary action. The principal in question was not in Cherokee ry long.

At least one man probably noticed what they were doing, and when the mmer came for Mary to retire, then-Principal Sam Hyatt asked Mary and Nan ner to make copies of their Cherokee materials to be available in all the assrooms of the school.

Mary says it is ironic that since Franklin Delano Roosevelt had had the wisdom to appoint the eccentric John Collier to head the Bureau of Indian Affairs these Reconstruction laws had long before that distressing day been changed and amended.

Mary is named Woman of the Week by the Asheville ***Citizen****; she is shown holding her carving of St. Francis of Assisi and with G.B.'s famous buffalo and others of his carvings. (Photograph by Malcolm Gamble)*

Wild about Books and Flowers

Also at about the time *Unto These Hills* was being developed, George Stephens suggested a need for a collection of recipes from the cooks on the Boundary who still knew the old ways. Mary and G.B. worked together with publisher Samuel Beck putting together this first book, which was then called *To Make My Bread.* She says that working together on a book, even a cookbook, is a pretty good way to start courting.

In July 1951 the book, now known as *Cherokee Cooklore*, was published. Mary was inexperienced in the frustrations of publication, and she says when the little book arrived at her door and she took a first look, she wanted to hide and cry. Forty years later, there is still a shudder when she remembers hiding the books in a back room and trying to forget they had ever happened.

The tourist trade in Cherokee was still in its infancy, and the cookbooks sold at a snail's pace. In fact, twenty years later, when her *Cherokee Words* book received a much more enthusiastic attention, the cookbook finally "took off," and both books are in steady demand even now.

Besides the collection of native recipes, including such unusual items as "Yellow Jacket Soup" and "Blood Pudding," the *Cooklore* includes a pictorial explanation of Aggie Lossiah's bean bread, an herbs list with medicinal uses, and the foods list from the Cherokee Indian Feast sponsored by the Museum of the Cherokee Indian on December 4, 1949.

In addition to her growing knowledge of Cherokee legends and cooking, Mary was developing an expertise in the wild flowers and mountain plants. Girl Scout troops and groups of all ages depended on Mary to take them into the mountains and help them learn the native plants with their area names and their scientific names. After the *Words* book, this interest also grew into a collaboration with Paul Hamel titled *Cherokee Plants.* The *Plants* book, published in 1975, listed native plants along with traditional uses of the plants.

Thousands of Girl Scouts, senior citizens, and lucky visitors to Cherokee have walked the trails and mountains around Western North Carolina to hear Mary Ulmer of West Alabama tell of the flowers and plants along the way.

When we were little brats in Marengo County, Alabama, we eagerly awaited the walks with Aunt Mary to dig down in the leaves to find the little pitchers of the heart plants. I think we thought she was magic and probably the little tuberous pitchers were there only because she was there. Later, she told us how to select the sweetwater stream if we should want to set up a moonshine still (we found this ironic since Mary is a strict "tee-totaller"), and she took us up to where the blueberries grew shoulder high in the Smokies. In my mind I still look above blueberry thickets to see my Uncle Goingback walking above us on a mountain ridge, picking from the highest blueberry bushes in the world.

Gene Jackson's beautiful little granddaughter Skye Littledave now involves Mary in what she calls a "piggramage." Each season they take a nature walk to see how the plants change around Cherokee.

Delores West and Vickie Sequoyah McCoy both remember unusual Girl Scou trips with Mary as their fearless leader. On one such trip to Columbus, Georgia, anc Mobile, Alabama, they presented Cherokee stories and dances. During th friendship dance in Mobile, they danced with Will Rogers, Jr. Mary says the girl vowed never again to wash their hands! But let's not jump too far ahead. Betweei the *Cooklore* Book and *Words* book, Mary became Mrs. Goingback Chiltoskey.

Mary and G.B. stand in front of their home in Cherokee.

Haskell and Santa Fe

When we last left G.B., he had decided not to become a snake handler, and he was on his way back to Cherokee by way of Washington, D.C. From Cherokee he traveled on his own to Haskell Institute, a school for Indian students in Lawrence, Kansas. At Haskell, G.B. studied arts and crafts and carpentry with people from many Native American tribes. A brochure printed for Haskell's Centennial celebration in 1984 says that Haskell students represent 120 tribes from 37 of the United States.

At Haskell, Goingback got the appointment to work at a children's camp in Massachusetts. After that he was asked to teach at a camp in Pennsylvania and then other summer camps around the country. The little boy who grew up in the mountains was able to travel and teach Indian lore, stories, beadwork, and camping skills all over the nation. G.B. remembers that years before he was noticed for summer camp work at Haskell, he was invited during the summer after eighth grade in Cherokee to work at Camp Old Indian near Greenville, South Carolina. His assignment that summer was "to be an Indian at the camp!"

At one Scout camp in Pennsylvania, G.B. was assigned a select group of advanced Scouts to construct "a typical Indian camp." Years later, Carl Shook of Pennsylvania sought out G.B. at his home in Cherokee. Carl was one of those boys; years later he had brought his own Scout troop to learn about the Cherokee culture. Each year (since 1939) he still brings groups to study the dances of the Cherokee.

After finishing at Haskell, G.B. studied carpentry, silver smithing, Navajo jewelry techniques such as turquoise cutting and polishing, and stone and metal working at the American Indian Art Institute at Santa Fe, New Mexico. During his years studying in these western schools, G.B. met people from many North American tribes, and he saw their art and crafts and heard their stories.

When he finished his studies at Santa Fe, he was offered three jobs -- two out West and one back home in Cherokee. He was ready to go back home. So in 1935 he went back to Cherokee to begin the woodcarving and woodworking program at Cherokee High School. For the next eight years, the little boy who had come down from the mountains to learn a new way of life and language taught the children of Cherokee the woodcarving and woodworking he had begun to learn from Watty in his Cherokee home.

G.B. Chiltoskey was the 1995 nominee for Haskell Alumni of the Year from the Cherokee area.

Michelangelo of the Mountains

When Goingback came down from the mountain to learn English and the new ways, he brought with him his habit of whittling that he says is "a gift I'm thankful I have." He had watched Watty whittle, and he had started to carve small animals when he was very young. At the boarding school and later at Parker High he found that people would buy his wood carvings at a time when he needed to earn whatever money he had.

It was not long before his woodcarving brought him more than nominal recognition. At Haskell, he was in demand for camp work all over the country. He worked at camps teaching children the Cherokee crafts, and he studied woodworking, carving, and crafts of all kinds at Haskell, Santa Fe, and later at Oklahoma State University, Purdue University, Corcoran School of Art in Washington, D.C., and the Chicago Art Institute.

His talents were extraordinary, and his determination to learn and to teach was strong. During his years of teaching at Cherokee High School, he was invited to instruct a laboratory course in wood carving and jewelry making at Purdue University. Mike Bowen wrote in 1972, "Goingback Chiltoskey calls himself a woodcarver, but that is like calling Rembrandt a paint-user" (The Greenville *News*, 5-21).

Goingback teaches the way he sees things, carefully, without regard to the present time. He remembers seeing buffalo on a ranch in New Mexico, and he describes his way of looking at the animal. "I would go around and around the buffalo," he told me. "You know, when you see a picture of a buffalo, you don't see the buffalo because you don't see the thickness, the textures." He is frustrated sometimes when people ask him how long it takes to finish a carving because he doesn't deal in time and because he says there is not enough time to do all he wants to do.

One of his most famous early carvings is a buffalo he carved in the 1930's. This carving and several others from the early works can be seen in the Cherokee area. At the Museum of the Cherokee Indian near Qualla Arts and Crafts are his self-portrait and his bas-relief of a warrior and a canoe, both from the thirties. At Cherokee Hospital is G.B.'s Corn Maiden, another early bas-relief. Also in the Museum at Cherokee, visitors marvel at his large carved Seal of the Cherokee Nation. An early St. Francis of Assisi is owned by the Indian Arts and Crafts Board in Washington; another St. Francis can be seen at the Church of the Advent, Birmingham, Alabama.

Awards and commissions began to come his way during and after his eight years of teaching at Cherokee High School. Several of his carvings, including his famous Woman Carrying a Bundle and St. Francis of Assisi, were displayed at the Smithsonian Museums in Washington. He was awarded the first Purchase Award for woodcarving at the North Carolina Museum of Art for his great horned owl in 1954. In 1965 he was commissioned to carve a bust of Governor Zeb Vance for display at the birthplace in Weaversville.

Many articles have been written about this quiet, careful Cherokee artist. Writers, painters, sculptors, and journalists love to watch him work, ask him questions, and capture his likeness in oils, metals, words, and spirit. I tease him it's those wonderful eyebrows, but it's the craftsman who does his absolute best without regard to the whirl around him.

Wilma Dykesman of the Knoxville *News-Sentinel* wrote, "One could wish that he will someday sculpt his own likeness in walnut or cherry wood" (5-25-72). Among the many artists who have featured G.B. in their work are acclaimed Knoxville artist Hubert Shuptrine, whose watercolor and drybrush paintings of Goingback are published in his *Home to Jericho* (53-55), and Harmer Weichel of Cherokee, whose portrait of G.B. was commissioned for the Mariana Black Library in Bryson City. Greenville photographer Ted Ramsaur's photograph of G.B. was selected for the 1983 Southeastern Photography Exhibition, and William Paulk of Western Carolina University published his sonnet about G.B.'s eagle dance in *Appalachian Heritage* (see back cover). Visitors to the Museum of the Cherokee Indian can purchase delightful prints of Elizabeth McAfee's "Cherokee Storyteller" in which there are Sequoyah, Chief John Ross, G.B., and others cuddled in the arms of a mama bear!

G.B. told Ms. Dykesman that "If left to my 'druthers', I carve creatures of nature, especially the ones I knew as a boy" (5-25-72). He told me his carvings show how things used to be. He says the early carving of a woman with a bundle shows how the women, including his mother, always dressed. He points out how very different life and lifestyles are now. When G.B. was named Tarheel of the Week in 1973, he told reporter Ernie Wood, "When I was a child, I just had the habit of wanting to make things. As a child, you always wanted to have things - things to play with - and I never had much. So I had to make it."

In an Asheville *Citizen-Times* (1982) article about his accepting an honorary life membership in the International Wood Collectors Society, G.B. says, "A knife and a piece of wood were the material and tools that I had at hand. When an opportunity came to me to sell a piece of work, I felt the satisfaction that came from a boost to my economic condition. Any boy is happy to be able to have money in his pocket to buy a piece of candy when he wants it." He said as a boy he carved toy water wheels and animals and snakes on walking canes to "satisfy a longing for making something." He said, "The very simplest things of life were meaningful in those days."

A feature in Hendersonville's *Times-News* (4-2-76) says G.B. has been called "the Michelangelo of woodcarvers." That same year Carson Brewer wrote in the Knoxville *News-Sentinel:* "It just dawned on me that Goingback Chiltoskey must be able to do nearly anything that requires a skilled hand and a sharp eye" (10-21-76). In an article for the Asheville *Citizen-Times*, George Ellison writes about craftsman Hugh Lambert of Cherokee. Lambert was a student at the Cherokee School during the late thirties. Lambert says, "During my years at the Cherokee School, I studied with G.B. [Chiltoskey]. He taught me everything in that line I know. Sometimes now people look at one of my dulcimers and say, 'You're a master craftsman.' I have to say, 'No, I'm not, but I did learn from one.' "

Don Sturkey of the Charlotte *Observer* wrote (10-10-86): "He is respected throughout America and Europe for his museum quality wood sculpting." G.B. dismisses much of the praise with the classic woodcarver's explanation. "You look at a piece of wood until you see a bear or something you want in it," he says. "Then you cut away the excess wood and there is your bear."

Ever the optimistic teacher, G.B. would come to Alabama each Christmas supplied with wood-blocked ducks and dogs and bears for us nieces and nephews to learn to carve. Patiently, he would instruct and encourage until we had chopped off most of the heads, tails, and legs of our pieces of pre-art. I don't think he had ever seen animals like we made, and probably he has never seen any since those years.

Warren Moore, in her 1988 book *Mountain Voices*, quotes Mr. Bea Hensley, an internationally acclaimed craftsman of Gillespie Gap, North Carolina saying, "G.B. Chiltoskey is one of the greatest woodcarvers in the world . . . I've been fortunate to spend hours with him."

One of Goingback's prized carvings is the large replica of the Cherokee seal which he carved for the Museum of the Cherokee Indian. His careful work on the seal included making his own special tool to craft the leaves and the letters as part of the background. To prevent warping, he glued together several narrow boards, bored holes from side to side, put metal rods in the holes and plugged them so carefully with the same grain of wood that the work is a perfect match.

G.B. holds his eagle made of cherry wood.

Washington D. C. and Hollywood

In 1942 after eight years at Cherokee High School, Goingback applied for a position with the U.S. Army Corps of Engineers in Washington, D.C. He accepted a position with the Corps, but soon he was transferred to the War Department. He worked as a model maker in Fort Belvoir, Virginia, at what he describes as "one of the largest military divisions where soldiers learned war games."

The year was full of war plans, and G.B. worked on scale models of new inventions and invasion maps and bombing targets. He had left Cherokee in August, 1942, for D.C. a few days before a young woman from Alabama came to the village on the train. G.B. stayed with the Corps of Engineers for the nearly all of next 25 years.

An article by Wanda Crawford in *Appalachian Heritage* (Fall 1979) describes G.B.'s assignments in the Corps: "Chiltoskey's duties in the Civil Service involved making scale models of war inventions . . . Until the end of World War II, using experimental materials like fiberglass and plastic, he fabricated working models from plans of inventors, enlarging mechanisms and demonstrating the finished precision machine in front of large groups." Goingback made terrain maps for the invasions of Normandy and North Africa, and he modeled bombing targets of the South Pacific.

G.B. told Greenville *News* writer Mike Bowen, "We made the models from aerial photographs, most of which came from the British Royal Air Force. Most of the work was highly classified, because we were about six months ahead of the invasion forces. They warned us not to talk about the work to anyone, ... especially not women. That's what they told us" (5-21-72).

After the war was over, people were full of big new plans. In August, 1946, G.B. and some entrepreneurs set out for Hollywood to set up an "imagineering" business making models for movie sets. Among other projects in their eleven months in Tinsel Town, they made sets for the bird act known as "Bill and Coo" and the sets for the movie version of *The Black Rose*. Perhaps the most unusual model G.B. tells about is the model of an elephant made so that a live bird could act with it.

Soon G.B. was disillusioned with the fakery of Hollywood and in May of 1947, after a short time in Cherokee, he was back in Washington.

Bert Swenson, now living in Alexandria, Virginia, was G.B.'s supervisor when he returned to Fort Belvoir in 1947. Mr. Swenson, a native of Sweden, told me he was invited to go to Hollywood with his co-workers, but he had family responsibilities which kept him in Washington. He describes G.B. as a "special kind of craftsman." He would assign G.B. the unusual jobs ranging from relief maps of various theatres during World War II to city models of Hiroshima after the atomic bomb to models of water installations. He said that G.B. could carve anything from wood and make anything from metal. "G.B.," he said, "did the right kind of job. He is one of the best there is."

Mrs. Swenson said her children idolized G.B. when they were growing up. He would visit in their home and tell them about the Cherokee people.

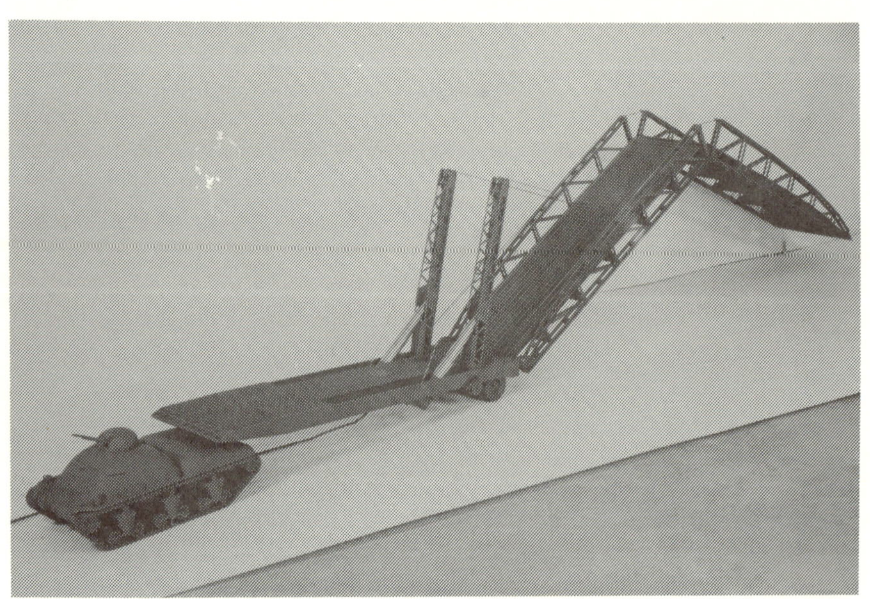

This is a model of an early version of a tank mounted portable bridge. A hydraulic version of this type of bridge is standard equipment with the army and was used in the late war "Desert Storm." Information from Bert Swenson. (U.S. Army Photo).

This is a model of a "Landing Ship, Tank" (designated LST by the military), a "workhorse" for transporting men and equipment to the war theatre. Information from Bert Swenson (U.S. Army Photo).

Goingback is in Washington with his model of the Fort Belvoir nuclear power plant and some of his carvings. (U.S. Army Photo)

Bert Swenson, G.B., and Walter Edwards put the finishing touches on a model of the "Landing Ship, Tank" (LST). (U.S. Army photo)

Love without Boundary

While Mary was becoming quite an authority on the Cherokee culture and a community leader and G.B. was off in the nation's capital working for the government, they were working together on books and projects when he came home to Cherokee. Mary even became a woodcarver (and took awards for her work) with a pocket knife G.B. gave her and his expert instruction.

Joan Greene, in an article for East Tennessee State University's **Now and Then** reports that in 1954 when G.B. was leaving to go back to Washington, Mary said, "I don't know if I'll be able to stay here with you gone."

"No matter where you go, I'll find you," G.B. answered her.

In 1946 G.B. made for Mary a pin of silver and ebony which she has worn since that day. While he was working on secret weapons at Fort Belvoir, G.B. met a visitor to the base who had some art made in Burma. It gave him the idea to do the pin in silver and ebony, and with the face of a Burmese woman. When he offered Mary an engagement ring, she said she already had the pin. And that has always been enough.

On a trip to Nashville to help make adjustments on the model of the spillway of Kentucky Dam, G.B. found time to make a wedding ring from Mary's great-grandmother's ring. When he returned to Cherokee, he gave the ring to Mary to "keep until we find a use for it." They began to make wedding plans only to find that marriage between a white person and an Indian was not a legal ritual in the state of North Carolina.

Mary has letters which she wrote to South Carolina, Tennessee, and North Carolina, in which she questioned the marriage laws. In both Carolinas, intermarriage between Indians and whites was illegal. After their marriage in Knoxville, Tennessee, Mary's associates in the League of Women Voters took her concerns to legislators in North Carolina, and in the next session of the legislature, the laws were amended.

Mary's aunt Clara Tucker remembers that her very first plane ride was to help Mary pick out her wedding dress.

Goingback and Mary were married in Knoxville on June 9, 1956, at St. John's Episcopal Church.

Mary told Sister Laurita from Nazareth College in a 1969 interview: "I came to Cherokee and taught the Indians and fell in love with one who taught me much more than I've ever taught anyone else." During the decade between their marriage and their retirements, Mary and G.B. had a commuter marriage long before it was fashionable. She taught the Cherokee children on the Qualla Boundary, and he worked for the American government in Washington.

G.B. says that Washington was getting "wicked" in the mid-sixties, and in 1966 he retired from government work to come back to build his home on his acres on the banks of the Oconaluftee. G.B. had planned his home with scale models for years, and now he would get to start to build their dream home.

G.B., Watty, and (r) Chief Owslie Saunooke work on carvings and chat at the Cherokee Fair. (Photo by Orin G. Foyle)

Home on the Oconaluftee

They had been married for eleven years when Mary retired from teaching in 1967. G.B. was in Cherokee, having retired from government service in 1966, and he was ready with full-scale plans for his house and land on the Oconaluftee. For many of the people who have found inspiration from the Chiltoskeys, the story begins here.

Instead of calm and slow retirement, both G.B. and Mary became involved in many activities around the Western Carolina area.

Cherokee needed a community library; Mary and her helpers including Virginia Million, Dee Smith, and Mollie Blankenship, got one started.

Churches and colleges needed sculpture by area masters for their halls and sanctuaries. G.B. produced busts, including one commissioned for the Governor Zeb Vance birthplace near Weaversville, and crosses and relief sculpture. One of the pieces is the tall Goddess of Justice which G.B. finished in 1980 for Campbell University School of Law.

Cherokee artists needed an outlet for the mountain arts and crafts. G.B. was a charter member of the cooperative named Qualla Arts and Crafts, which has grown to be a model for cooperatives around the country. He told Carolanne Griffith for a *Southern Living* article (September, 1986), "Our craftspeople needed a reason to continue with their crafts, a place where the crafts could be appreciated and seen. Only the members of the tribe may belong - today there are around 300" (75). In May 1972 he opened a one-man exhibit which was displayed for two months at Qualla Arts and Crafts.

During the sixties, tour groups were flooding into Cherokee to see *Unto These Hills*, the Oconaluftee Indian Village, the Museum of the Cherokee Indian, the Cherokee Cyclorama and Wax Museum and many other attractions. People had questions about the Cherokee culture, which had at times seemed in danger of being lost. Visitors found out the Chiltoskeys could answer your question, or they could help you find the answer. They also found out that if you have a question for Mary Chiltoskey, you had better be ready for a complete answer, and not necessarily a predictable one. In a 1969 interview, Mary said the tribal set-up of the Eastern Band of the Cherokee is "the most democratic organization that you will find in the United States."

In the early 1970s some of the educators in Cherokee became determined that the children should have the opportunity to learn the old language. Rev. G. George and kindergarten teacher Claudia Webb and others started a class in the kindergarten to help the children begin to learn about the language which Sequoyah had written down 140 years before. The classes heard the language spoken and sung, and they learned Cherokee songs, but they needed a book to use.

Will West Long of Big Cove, who had been an early teacher of the Cherokee language at Cherokee High School, had done much research on a dictionary of Cherokee words, but he died before he got a chance to finish his work. Long left his research to George Stephens, who made it available to Mary. Claudia Webb and

Mary, with the help of G.B., Watty Chiltoskie, and Virginia Million, began to work on a little book of Cherokee words. In the evenings after supper, they would discuss which words and phrases the children would need to know. Watty could read and write Cherokee, and he and G.B. had spoken only Cherokee in their childhood home in the mountains.

In January 1972 Mary dedicated the new *Words* book to "the memory of Sequoyah and Will West Long, to the patience of Watty and Goingback and to my cats who kept me from working too long at one time." In the book she included a page from Long's work, one of Will West Long's letters, the hymn in Cherokee ("Amazing Grace") which Tsali is said to have requested before he face the firing squad to die for his people, and simple information about the Cherokee as well as words and phrases with pronunciation and Cherokee characters.

A contest was held to determine who would illustrate the little book. This task went to Lib Lambert, art teacher at the Cherokee school. Ms. Lambert's dozens of illustrations have delighted many readers of the *Words* book.

G.B. became active in the Southern Highland Handicraft Guild and later in the International Wood Collectors Society. G.B. and Mary both attended the first Craftsman's Fair in Gatlinburg in 1947. They were both elected life members of the Guild, and for many years (until his heart attack), they set up wood carving demonstrations and did story telling at the Fair. G.B. and Mary did more demonstrating than selling because since his first return from Haskell, his commissions have taken nearly all the work he could produce.

A member of the Guild, Miss Fannie Mennen, organized the famous Plum Nelly Art Show in the mountains above Trenton, Georgia. Miss Fannie asked the Chiltoskeys to bring over some Cherokee baskets when basket-making got scarce in the Georgia mountains. So Mary and G.B. bought up baskets and set up a booth at Plum Nelly. (I can't resist explaining that Plum-Nelly is said to mean "plum out of Tennessee and nelly out of Georgia.")

In 1978 Richard "Geet" Crowe brought a request from the Cherokee Fair and Festival Association that Mary put together a book abut the traditions of the Festival held each fall. In 1979 that project became Mary's fourth book about Cherokee. ("Geet" was an absolute hero to us Ulmer kids of West Alabama from the time of his acting in the Disney move *Davey Crockett, King of the Wild Frontier.* His Indian dance troupes have performed for fascinated crowds all over the Southeast.)

The 1979 book titled *A History of the Cherokee Fair and Festival thru 1978* tells of the Cherokee fall festivals from the first one held in 1914 on the Cherokee Indian School grounds through the renovation of the ceremonial grounds and exhibition mall made possible by a government grant in 1977. It includes the history of the parade, the games, the dances and music, and the "Miss Cherokee" and "Miss Fall Festival" selections. In an *Asheville Citizen-Time* article (9-30-79), Virginia Million writes that Mary was assisted by Beverly Korst, Goingback, Geet Crowe, and Cherokee *One Feather* editor Richard Welch in researching and editing the book.

In the years after retirement from teaching and government work, G.B. and Mary agreed to thousands of requests from groups all over the South to come and talk about Cherokee crafts, legends, and all parts of the Cherokee story. They were and still are combination missionary-ambassadors for the culture they know and love.

Most of the engagements Mary and G.B. have accepted have been school groups, church groups, groups of Scouts or senior citizens, or other groups who have visited the Great Smokies area. But two of the groups are among those which were quite unusual.

In January 1977 the Chiltoskeys were invited to speak to some children down in the southernmost part of Louisiana, Cajun country. They were invited to Du Lac, Louisiana, to do a community crafts program for an area technical school. Mary says this was quite a challenging assignment because these children of the marsh-lands had no idea at all of hills, much less mountains, and so many of the Cherokee legends depend on the tall trees and the mountain terrain. That January day, something extraordinary happened. It snowed in Du Lac, Louisiana! Maybe the Chiltoskeys brought the snow from those mountains.

Another unusual session happened in the Federal Prison in Atlanta in 1976. Mary and G.B. had been invited to come tell stories and Cherokee culture because some of the inmates, who were Cherokee, had a chance to request the program. These men were, of course, trapped in prison, and they apparently had to come to the program, if they got to do anything at all. One haughty white-collar inmate saw no use in listening to Indian stories, and he showed his displeasure by sitting stiffly in the seat the guard made him take. Mary says she watched him all during the session, and, little by little, his stone face melted and he got into these old tales just like she has watched people of all ages and situations react. After the program, the "haughty man" waited to shake hands and chat after the other inmates left.

Some of Mary and G.B.'s prized treasures are the many letters they have received from school children who have heard their programs. Laura from Dickson, Tennessee, wrote, "My favorite part was when you taught the legends, that's not to mention how you made people feel right when you say, 'You're right, there's more to it,' it really makes people feel like they got it right."

Allen from Dickson wrote, "I learned a whole lot from you. A lot of people would of got board, but I sure didn't."

A favorite of the hundreds of letters came from Keisha from Smokey Mountain School. She wrote, "I would like to thank you for the legends you told. And for setting us straight on legends, stories, and falsehoods. Sometimes I wish that I knew more about Indians and their way. I can't explain it but when I hear a legend I want to hear it over and over again."

*G.B. is featured by The **State** demonstrating carving to an interested youngster at the Craftman's Fair in 1953.*

The Book Lady Becomes An Indian

In the early eighties Mary received a call from Boys Club Director Ray Kinsland bringing a message from Chief Robert Youngdeer. The chief asked her to go to Reno, Nevada, to represent the Eastern Band at a meeting about books. The catch was that they had to decide by the next morning at 8:15. On Sunday, December 9, 1983, G.B. and Mary left for Reno to represent the Eastern Band of the Cherokee at a workshop about a free book program approved by the IRS. Mary, always one to love a challenge, came back to Cherokee with a plan to distribute free books to qualifed area citizens. A certain number of books would be available free of charge to children, the ill, the elderly, and citizens considered isolated from books.

The morning after the Chiltoskeys flew back from Reno, they were called to the office of Mr. Muskrat, supposedly to talk about their trip. The surprise was that two **large** loads of books had already arrived and were being loaded into the building provided for the Free Book Center. By December 20, the books were processed to the point that the first books could be issued to Brian and Becky Ensley, then 10 and 8 years old. The Book Center was required to report to the director Dr. Max Celnik on the first Tuesday in January that they had given out at least one book: When Mary called Dr. Celnik in Long Island that morning, the total was over 20,000 books given to over 5,000 people!

Gene Jackson remembers the afternoon that her granddaughter Skye, at that time five years old, brought her first four books from the Free Book Center. Skye had Gene begin to read to her immediately, and after three of the four books, Gene said, "Skye, it's getting late. We can read the other book tomorrow. You have to get up early for school."

"No," Skye insisted. "We have to read it tonight. You know, your old grandmother will give us some more books tomorrow!"

Books on all subjects and for all ages have been available to the citizens of Cherokee because Mary has a passion for books. Many of the children who are too young to have been Mary's students consider her the Book Lady.

In 1990 the Cherokee center, easily the most active in the country, documented the distribution of the **one millionth book**! The millionth volume was given to Mrs. Sarah Catt Owl. I tease Mary that most of these books were probably required reading, since she has taught many of the recipients and their parents.

Mary had anticipated the millionth book for weeks, even months. Now, when the book was ready to be distributed, she was in a little bit of a quandary. The cover of the book and the content of the book involve a sexual situation which makes many people nervous. Now, Mary is a librarian, and they do not like censorship of any kind. Also, as she explained to me, "Many times a story is just the truth." When the truth is controversial or uncomfortable, I have heard Mary explain, "It may not be normal, but it surely is natural."

She pondered and argued inside, and she decided to take the cover from the book because "that's not really the book," but she would distribute the book as is. The millionth book was *I, Eve* by Edward LeComte. A year after the millionth book on July 16, 1991, the number had grown to 1,078,824!

The book center project meant Mary and faithful volunteers like Mrs. Raye Seay, Mrs. Margaret Owle, and Mr. and Mrs. Wallace Calhoun, manned the center nearly fulltime for over seven years (of retirement?). Mary's work at the Book Center has meant daily hours of work and influence on area citizens. It has also meant recognition for her persistent interest in education for the Cherokee area.

In a May 1991 letter to Mary, Linda Campbell describes the varied blessings of the book center: "Now I have books I can read at my leisure and share with my friends and neighbors." Ms. Campbell tells of a neighbor from Korea who is reading to master the English language, neighborhood children who are learning to value books, and a college student who "found many books at the Center which were of great help in pursuing her education to become a teacher."

In 1987 Mary accepted an award as a Distinguished Woman of North Carolina given to five outstanding women by the North Carolina Council on the Status of Women. She told me she felt so much tension around her at the luncheon that when her name was called, she just went right up and gave North Carolina Governor Martin a big kiss. Then she looked at the audince and said, "Ladies, anytime you kiss a married man, you'd best be just as willing to kiss his wife." Then she went over and planted a big kiss and hug on Mrs. Martin.

In her nomination of Mary for the Distinguished Woman designation, Mollie Blankenship wrote "Mrs. Chiltoskey became so interested in the Cherokee people that she began collecting Indian legends, became an authority on native herbs and wild flowers, and compiled a number of recipes for Cherokee foods . . . In addition to all her other collecting since coming to Cherokee, she has collected a Cherokee Indian husband, Mr. Goingback Chiltoskey, noted wood sculptor."

Ray Kinsland, General Manager of the Cherokee Boys Club, Inc., and longtime friend of the Chiltoskeys wrote "[Mary] has probably done more than anyone else in preserving our history and culture and in teaching it to others."

In 1989 members of the Eastern Band of the Cherokee invited Mary Ulmer of Alabama to become an honorary Cherokee. She accepted with tears in her eyes at a ceremony and luncheon on Thursday, April 6, 1989; her Cherokee name is **Ah-hi-ga-li-ya Ah-tsi-nv-si-ea-sdi** which means **dedicated servant.** Former student and longtime companion Geneva Jackson said, "Nobody remembered she wasn't a member. Nobody has contributed like she has" (Asheville *Citizen-Times*, 4-989).

A resolution was read that day in April which cited Mary's contributions as "teacher, librarian, author, volunteer, community leader, and 'ambassador of good will'." In *Blue Ridge Country* (Fall 1990), Helen Barranger describes Mary as a lady "bright as a new penny, sharp as a tack, quick as a fox, enthusiastic as a puppy."

Mary stands ready to distribute books at the Free Book Center in Cherokee.

Mary and G.B. pose with his Goddess of Justice commissioned for Campbell College School of Law, Buies Creek, North Carolina. (Photo by Campbell College)

A Snake in the Garden

In May 1988, G.B. was out in his beautiful garden near the home in Cherokee when it seemed that the story was coming to an end. Henry Chiltoskey's little daughter Rachel saw G.B. lying in the corn, and called to her daddy. Henry yelled to Alva Crowe who called to Geet and Berdina who called the rescue squad.

Gene Jackson remembers that she was returning from a relief assignment as school nurse at Cherokee High School when she drove into the Chiltoskey driveway and saw G.B. lying in the garden. Gene says she could at first get no vital signs, but after a little work, she felt a tiny heartbeat. Gene picked him up and put him in the rescue van, which had arrived in minutes. Gene called "Code Blue" in to the Cherokee hospital, and she says that all the hospital was on alert when they arrived there, minutes later.

G.B. was stabilized and flown by Air-Vac helicopter to ICU at Memorial Mission Hospital in Asheville. Dr. John Lawrence credits Gene with taking the steps necessary to prevent loss of oxygen to the brain, so G.B.'s recovery has seemed miraculous. G.B. had suffered a stroke and was left with heart blockage of 70%. Gene says G.B.'s life was saved by Skilly French and Ned Stamper's fast and efficient EMT response and by the perfect response of everyone at Cherokee Hospital.

G.B., Mary, and Gene did not give up. Mary and Gene helped G.B. gradually regain his strength and learn to regulate his medicine and diet. Wood carving projects had to be delayed a while. G.B. had, a few years before, made a lion for the president of the International Lions Club. At the time of his heart attack, he had been working on a lion to present to the North Carolina Lions Club President. G.B.'s and Amanda Crowe's former student, acclaimed carver Virgil Ledford finished the project while G.B. was recuperating.

One part of G.B.'s life has seemed most important after his serious illness. In 1982 he accepted the honor of life membership in the International Wood Collectors Society. In this organization he has contact with people all over the world who love, collect, and work with woods. G.B. has made a display for the IWCS of hearts and wood samples which use 26 woods which are available within two miles of his home in Cherokee. He has written a paper giving the names and information about uses of the twenty-six woods. G.B. has carved pieces using each of these woods and several more available near the Chiltoskey home.

A goal in the year of convalescing was to attend the National Convention of the Wood Collectors to be held in Williamsport, Pennsylvania. Though it seemed an impossible dream, he went to Williamsport, and he hasn't missed an annual convention since.

This year, on the set of the feature film of James Fenimore Cooper's novel *The Last of the Mohicans*, G.B. played a revered Mohawk elder. When the days were long and hot and lunch was delayed for hours, he sat through costuming and went through days of shooting without a sign of complaint.

That would have surprised me more if I had not arrived to see how he was doing during the summer of 1990, two years after the near-fatal stroke. There was G.B. demonstrating for a television film crew how to hit the bulls-eye with his blowgun. G.B., who had been blowgun champion for ten straight years during his 60s and 70s, was still at it at 83.

One of the famous episodes from Cooper's novel has the hero Hawkeye hitting a buried bullet which is in the center of a bulls-eye. You won't believe this, but it is true: G.B. actually does have in his dining room a dart from a blowgun which he shot into another dart which was in the bulls-eye! The American hero lives and is well in Cherokee.

G.B. holds the blowgun before competing at the Cherokee Festival.

G.B.'s altar cross made of poplar was commissioned for Oak Forest Presbyterian, West Asheville. The arms of the cross were made to curve to the same degree as the altar walls. (Photo by U.S. Department of the Interior Arts and Crafts Board)

The Myth Is A True Story

In 1990 several things happened that were milestones: Mary and the book center volunteers distributed the one millionth book, the outdoor drama *Unto These Hills* dedicated their forty-first season to Mary and G.B. Chiltoskey for their long devotion to saving the culture of the Cherokee, and people asked Mary repeatedly, "When are you going to write down the stories?"

There were several problems with writing down the stories. For one, the Cherokee lore has, for most of history, been within an oral culture. Sequoyah's historic syllabary, which allowed the writing of the Cherokee language, happened only a few years before the terrible Trail of Tears, in which much of the Cherokee culture was uprooted and driven to the West.

The stories have lived and changed as surely as individuals have lived and changed, and writing them seems to freeze the change. One of the members of the Eastern band told me during the writing of the legend book that "writing the story kills the storyteller." These stories belong in a sense to the mountains and the smoke and the feelings of the people about whom they are told. Most of the culture lived in memory, not on the printed page.

Another problem for Mary was that when she wrote down the legends she told so freely, she felt them get flat and die. Perhaps the stories lost their living water like the pumped water is not the same as the flowing creeks of the legends, and perhaps Mary lost her own living in the legends when she wrote them for people not yet born.

In June 1990 I called Mary to tell her we had been transferred to Atlanta. I had delayed calling for several weeks because of hurry and something just would not let me call. When I told her, she said, "I knew you would call today and I knew it would have something to do with Atlanta." What? I thought, but I was not terribly surprised because Mary is in touch with more than just today, and sometimes she knows things in advance. It seemed to both of us that the next sentence was preordained: "I have to do something about these stories. People are asking me several times a day about them and I can't do anything about it."

I had never thought of a legends book: I had known for years that I was supposed to write a book about Mary and G.B., but frankly I'm a combination of lazy and scared, and I pushed this book aside with many excuses. On the telephone that day in May, 1990, I said, "It's time for the book." I meant the legends book about which I had never thought before. In researching this little biography, I have found that Mary described the legends book twenty years ago. She is a master teacher, and that means she knows when a lesson is right to be taught. By Groundhog's Day, 1991, *Aunt Mary, Tell Me A Story* was ready to be introduced to the Cherokee community.

In the *Legends* book, Mary explains that legends and myths are stories that are true. She insists a legend lives because it has truth, and when the truths die, the legend dies. A legend is not the same for all audiences; it is told to meet the needs of the group at the time. Little ears need different stories than adult ears, and situations can change the story but not the truth of the story. Legends from an oral culture like the Native American cultures lived in the memories of people who had needed the story at some time to explain a situation or a mystery. Other writers speak of a major creation myth, much of which has been lost. Surely some of the legends still repeated on the Qualla Boundary are remnants of this old wisdom.

The legends that Mary has heard and told during her fifty years in Cherokee seem to appeal to all ages. Since the book has been in circulation, we have received numerous letters from all over the country saying the book "talks" to them. They love Spearfinger, the demon who poses as a grandmother to snare little girls for their livers, Old Flint who is defeated by the crafty rabbit, the buzzard whose wings created the Smoky Mountains, and the fussy chiefs who hung the selfish smoke in the first place. I love the mean trick by which the poor 'possum lost his tail, and the sad, heroic tale of the baby and the mud-turtle (saligugi).

Mary has told the stories to hundred of thousands of all kinds of people; she has also quilted the legends and the symbols and plants, especially the trees around Cherokee. Mary had always done sewing and weaving and quilting (She remembers working on a little quilt when she was four years old!), but when G.B. was accepted into the International Woodcollectors Society and when the Book Center was so successful, she found two good reasons for new quilts. She quilted the trees of the world for the wood collectors meetings, and she quilted the legends, block by block of story-pictures. She worked with Margaret Owle and Dee Smith on a quilt based on some of the Book Center book covers for presentation to Dr. Max Celnik, head of the Free Book Program. Many people around Western North Carolina have taken up quilting because Mary Chitoskey said, "Yes, it can be done."

One unusual quilt made in 1978 was used to raise money for the Cherokee Children's Home. Interested people from Cherokee and all around the country donated money to have their signatures embroidered on the quilt which was decorated by pieced seven-pointed stars designed by G.B. to commemorate the seven clans of the Cherokee. The quilt was then raffled off and won by a lady whose children have since then returned the quilt to Mary. My brother Dr. M.B. Ulmer has the quilt as part of his Cherokee collection.

In 1988 Mary's "Smokey Mountains Child's Quilt" was selected for exhibition in the second annual Great Smokies Art Show sponsored by the Museum of the Cherokee Indian. The Child's Quilt, which features symbols from "the legends, history, nature, and geography of the Qualla Indian Boundary" (36), is featured in *Quilts from Appalachia* published by Patricia Miner Macneal and Maude Southwell Wahlman for Penn State University and Palmer Museum of Art. This quilt is a part of Mary's niece Dorothy Howington's collection.

G.B. is especially proud of Mary's quilts; as he told me. "I remember my mother had a stack of quilts as high as my head."

At the legends book autograph session at Qualla Arts and Crafts, are Regina Galloway and Mary, who wrote the book, and G.B. and Bart Galloway, who illustrated it. (Photo by Johnny Galloway)

The World Comes Calling

The Chiltoskey home has been a meeting place for people with all kind of interests. Are you writing a book? painting a picture? sculpting? researching a feature? trying to figure out your new sawmill? making a video? finding yourself? finding your roots? learning to quilt? Someone will direct you to Goingback and Mary Chiltoskey. For example, tonight as I was writing at the Chiltoskey home, I answered the phone. It was a lady who lives in France and who is visiting in Virginia. Someone said she should visit the Chiltoskeys in Cherokee before she does her doctoral work on Cherokee writers. Mary came back into the house from visiting a neighbor, called the lady, and talked to her as if she had known her all her life.

When you arrive at the Chiltoskey home, you may run into many people from many places and, until recently, many cats. Mary and her good friend Virginia Million were known for years for their work with books and cats, lots of cats. It's sad for many of us that, since this spring, the cat era has passed, and Virginia, who died in 1982, is not still in Cherokee. But the Chiltoskey complex is still buzzing with activities.

Recently, in the middle of writing this book, Mary called me and said, "What are you doing around the 4th of July?"

"I don't know," I said. "Probably a little barbeque and fire works, why?"

"G.B. has been asked to be in a movie in Asheville," she said. "They are filming *The Last of the Mohicans*. G.B. will get to be one of the grandfathers!"

What an astonishing and ironic opportunity for an American literature teacher! I gasped, "Can I be your driver?"

So Tuesday, July 2, 1991, Mary, G.B., and I set out for Camp Adventure near Old Fort, North Carolina, so Goingback Chiltoskey of Cherokee could play a revered Mohawk elder in James Fenimore Cooper's story of the French and Indian War.

Camp Adventure turned out to be backwoods, snakey, and challenging, and the days of filming were long, hot, and tiring for everyone. G.B. at 84 stood long hours of costuming, traveling, and makeup like he had been a star all of his life. The picture of him in the middle of a cabin scene dressed in the loincloth, leggings, and feathered headress of a Mohawk elder was American enough for any fourth of July.

On the set G.B. enjoyed talking to people from the Mohawks and Senecas of New York state, an Oklahoma member of the Chickasaw tribe, and other Cherokee people who were in the movie. From Cherokee there were Walker Calhoun, George Squirrel, Maybelle McDonald (who is well-known for her years with *Unto These Hills*), and Elizabeth Calonahuskie. Some of the Mohawks from New York told us stories about being required to forget the old ways, including their native language, which were similar to what happened in Cherokee.

Mohicans was not G.B.'s first experience in moviemaking. Besides the many filmed television reports and documentaries he has been sought out for, he and Watty and others from Cherokee participated in a movie with Johnny Cash about the Trail of Tears, which was filmed near the Chiltoskey home in Cherokee.

G.B. waits at the base camp of the movie set for ***The Last of the Mohicans****. A member of the Oklahoma Choctaw tribe and Maybelle McDonald wait with him. G.B. and Walker play Mohawk elders, and Maybelle is G.B.'s movie wife. (Photo by Regina Galloway)*

BETTER THAN SANTA CLAUS: Giving All Year Long

The Chiltoskey story is like a Christmas shop which is open all the year, except they are always giving, not selling. Our Christmases started in West Alabama when we were little kids out on a farm-to-market road at the moment that Aunt Mary and G.B. drove up D.D. Mama's driveway. We pounced on them, asking for stories and little stuffed bears from Cherokee, Indian dolls, and carving models which G.B. brought to teach us.

I think the grown-ups waited just as excited as we did for my daddy's big sister, who always brought him a "chocolate pie kit" and good arguments about everything from raising children to the world situation. Daddy took G.B. hunting with him down in the swampland near Jefferson, Alabama, and I think the grown-up hunters became little awed boys when this tall, dark, silent Indian was among them.

A local legend says that on the first hunt, when a neighbor Bill Eddins was explaining to G.B. about setting out the deer stands around where the dogs would run, he said, "Mr. Chiltoskey, you'll stand at number seven."

The story grew that G.B., who hadn't said anything until then, said, "I stand here."

Eddins looked way up at this tall hunter and said, "Okay, Mr. Chiltoskey, you can stand anywhere you want to."

When the other hunters brought in trophy bucks and tales of the ones that got away, G.B. also brought perfectly carved deer made from a knot of wood found near his stand. My brother M.B., who hunted with the men from the age of 6, said that he would watch how G.B. hunted. "He wouldn't look around him like we would," M.B. told me. "He would sit and become a part of the whole environment, not needing to move his head or to move at all."

We knew that G.B. went into the mountains hunting bear and wild boar just like we thought Indians would know how to do.

For a time in the 70 s and 80 s, the Chiltoskey home really had its own Santa Claus. Roy Schultz had come to Cherokee to play Ole King Cole at Santa Land. He met Mary and G.B. and became a regular visitor. Later, Roy took the job of Santa Claus in North Pole, New York, and he even changed his name to Santa C. Claus. All year round he dressed in red, drove a big red Pontiac, and played the part on television and everywhere he went. We and our children were awed that Mary and G.B. were even befriending and advising Santa Claus, but really we weren't surprised.

I found that the people of Cherokee felt the same awe at the giving says of Mary and G.B. Gene Jackson says, "Everything I know, she [Mary] taught me, everything that means anything." She describes Mary's involvement with her Cherokee class of 1948 (Mary's first homeroom) as including manners "from picnics to banquets," citizenship (She took us to our first council meeting and took us to vote the first time), concern for others, and a determination to achieve.

When after high school Gene was too young to get into nurses training, Mary vouched for her, helped her apply, and paid her first year's tuition. "She never required anything except that I pass," Gene says, "but I graduated with the second highest score on the state nursing exam."

G.B.'s students like Hugh Lambert remember a teacher who did not talk except when it was needed. "When he said it," Lambert, an accomplished dulcimer maker, told me, "it was to the point." He said that, unlike regular woodworking classes, in G.B.'s class he learned jewelry making, using silver, turquoise, and copper, wrought iron work, and wood carving. He remembers that their first project was a little crouched rabbit like the ones in the mountains. G.B. made his own tools to meet his needs, and he would let the students work with his personal tools.

Mary speculates that the Cherokee boys have been known for excellent woodcarving possibly because the men had to make all the utensils needed around the home. But G.B.'s students were not all boys. His niece Amanda Crowe was also his student, and now she is among the most celebrated of the native American carvers. Amanda teaches woodcarving at Cherokee High School.

Mary and G.B. have never had children of their own, and yet they probably have as many children of their own as anyone. Mary has taught nearly everyone and their parents in Cherokee. G.B. has taught the area woodcarvers and anyone else who has wanted to know about the ways of the Cherokee.

In 1958 Mary's youngest sister Mariana died suddenly after surgery and left three small children. In the years following their mother's death, Dorothy, David, and Douglas Coats spent time living with their Aunt Mary and Uncle G.B. Dorothy lived with the Chiltoskeys during her junior and senior years of high school, and during her college years at Carson Newman, she considered Cherokee home. Dorothy's two children, Jennifer and Timothy Howington, are sources of special pride for Mary and G.B.

But before Mariana's death, Mary had quietly sent money home to the family, whether she had enough for herself or not. When she needed clothes, she made over whatever was not being used for someone else. Any number of times, I have been present when someone quietly saw Mary for a loan, and she very quietly helped them. She told me one time when we were discussing her sister Kitty, who had been an Episcopal missionary in Virginia, that perhaps Mary was to be a missionary outside the church. Mary is an active Episcopalian, having represented the church in national meetings when the church began to allow women to participate fully.

Mary sees needs, and she tries to meet them. She told me one time that so many differences are matters of geography that one should not split hairs about such things as religious terminology or what parts of life are "real." She explained to us how the Cherokee looked to the heavens with open eyes when they prayed to the Great One. She explained to us that the Eastern Cherokee do not live on a reservation. The name Cherokee Indian Reservation is a name used for the Qualla Boundary because visitors recognize it.

When people were wringing their hands about the "crass commercialism" of some of the shopping areas of Cherokee, Mary made costumes for people so they could make much-needed money during the summer tourist rush. She and G.B. also supported, at the same time, the more traditional and historic activities like the Oconaluftee Village and the drama.

G.B. told Caroleanne Griffith about the change that came to Cherokee when roads were built. "There were no roads here, just us and the Smokies. And what do you expect without roads? No people in and out. " After the thirties, he explained, there were roads and the national park and the Blue Ridge Parkway. "The people here were only too glad to share their heritage. Instead of being an invasion of outsiders, they served to help us recapture our own culture" (*Southern Living*, September 1986, 74).

When our son Cole was 5, he was absolutely engrossed in the sights and sounds of the tourist village in Cherokee. He saw Indians in big headdresses, and he ran into G.B.'s living room yelling, "Hey, G.B., I saw a real Indian!"

Through the years Mary and G.B. have been sought out for various recognitions of their work. In 1986 Western Carolina University Chancellor Myron Coulter presented Mary the Mountain Heritage Award on the college's annual Mountain Heritage Day. In his presentation, Dr. Coulter said, "Starting with a few books in a virtually empty room, she built a collection that includes authentic Cherokee legends and lore, a part of the culture that until then was largely unrecorded in writing. She did this against considerable odds, even in defying orders to throw out the Cherokee material she had gathered... for most of her life [Mary] has led the way in preserving for modern peoples the cultural heritage of the Cherokee Indians."

Dr. Coulter said that recognition of Mary was recognition of all the people in Cherokee who have worked so hard to support and encourage her efforts to preserve the Cherokee culture. "Without you," he told Mary, "a significant part of our heritage would have disappeared" (John Parris, "Roaming the Mountains," *Asheville Citizen-Times* 9-28-86).

In 1987 Mary was named one of the Distinguished Women of North Carolina. In a letter supporting her nomination, Rev. James Sequoyah, one of Mary's students in her first homeroom, wrote, "Mary practically raised the class of 1955 . . . She helped me and about 95% of other Indian children graduate from high school, through her dedication to teaching and her love for the Indian children" (11-25-86).

In 1990 Mary received the coveted Frell Owl Award in local recognition of her many years of working for the Cherokee people. When she was asked to come over to the Boys Club on the morning the award was presented, she thought that she was being asked to serve on the committee to determine who should receive the annual award. She sat down, realized what was happening, and said, "I could do nothing but put my head down and start bawling."

Mary also received the John Henry Award for her work on ethnic history in the Appalachians and much acclaim from area groups and organizations.

On her 84th birthday the Cherokee Indian School Class of 1948, Mary's first homeroom, honored her with a birthday dinner. Her gift was an Indian Head penny from her birth year 1907. The *One Feather* (Feb. 1991) printed Henry Stewart's poem "Mary Ulmer Chiltoskey" about Mary's contributions in which he wrote

"Mary is . . .
Much beloved by her husband G.B.
Much admired by the Cherokee people and others.
Much concerned about the deeply religious stance.

. . . .
Much engrossed in the welfare of the Cherokee people.
Much acquainted with human need.
And Much, Much more to all those who know and love her."

Mary told Eunice Fisher for a recent *Asheville Citizen Times* feature (8-8-91) that she sees so many of the Cherokee people and remembers them as eager students in her classes. Ms. Fisher writes, "At a recent dedication of the Cherokee Hospital helicopter pad, [Mary] said she had taught or seen all of those present at the school library at some time during her teaching years." Remembering her school library years, she told me about once finding a piece of bacon in a library book! "I always taught students to take care of their books," she said. She remembers the little girl from Big Cove, who probably just didn't want to eat all her breakfast and forgot about hiding the bacon, scrubbing that book until there was a hole where the bacon had been. (Whoever you are, don't feel alone: She taught me a few definite lessons, too.)

Goingback has been surprised and happy with his many recognitions. In addition to the first Purchase Award for wood carving by the North Carolina Museum of Art, he was chosen as an exhibitor at the America Discovers Indian Art Show held at the Smithsonian Institute in 1967. In 1982 he was recognized for service to the North American Indian Women's Association; in 1979 he was named a Kentucky Colonel! A Cherokee *One Feather* article by Virginia Million reports that General George Stewart, presenting the commission for Governor Julian Carroll of Kentucky, "commented on Chiltoskey's long record of service to his tribe and his community, his dedication to preservation of mountain heritage and his efforts in passing his wood carving skills on to younger people."

G.B. received the Western North Carolina Historical Association Achievement Award in 1974. He has been listed in *Dictionary of International Biography* (1977) and *Personalities of the South* (1976). Articles featuring G.B.'s work and his life story can be found in *Southern Living* (9-86), *Foxfire* (Summer 1981 and Fall 1983), *Journal of Cherokee Studies* (Spring 1986), *The State* (7-11-53), *National Geographic*, and *Holiday Magazine*, among others. (See chapter 10 for more about other artists' work.)

The story continues. At 84, neither Mary nor G.B. is slowing down. G.B.'s nephew Henry Chiltoskey and his family are building a home near Mary and G.B. Gene's grandchildren live with the Chiltoskeys much of the year. Gene declares that just the other day (August, 1991) she watched Mary being taught how to skateboard by Storm Toineeta, two-year old son of Sheila and Gary. If we can believe Gene, there was Mary holding her hands just right and skate-boarding all the way across her living room after watching Storm's demonstration. Jamie Jenks, hearing of Mary's new hobby, told Gene, "What we have here is a skateboarding granny!"

Program requests are pouring in. Visitors are calling and dropping by, and most of the time, the answer is Yes, the artist and the storyteller are at home, and if you need them, you are at home, too.

It is an American legend, being carved, quilted, watched, and told. It is a strong story being lived on the beautiful Oconaluftee River in the Great Smoky Mountains in the magic of the Qualla Boundary, Cherokee, North Carolina.

Mary and Beverly Korst illustrated the nine states within the Southern Highland Handicraft Guild region with this commemorative quilt.

Photo by Jennie Lea Knight

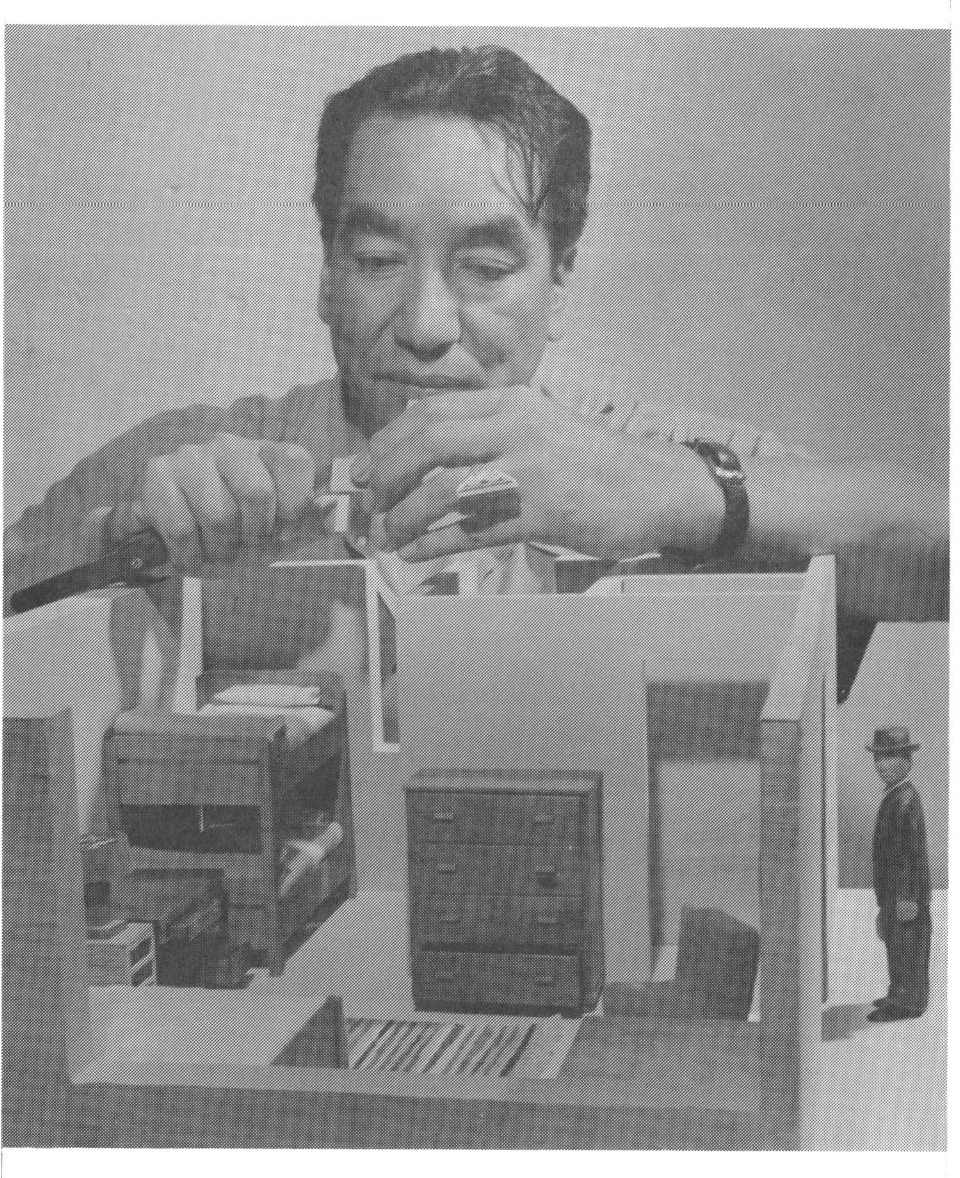

G.B. designs models of furniture for Boundary Tree Motor Court.
(1948 photo by N.J. Norman)